Also by Sarah Stup

Do-si-Do with Autism

are your eyes listening?

sarah stup
collected works

Are your eyes listening?
Sarah Stup, Collected Works

Copyright © 2007 Sarah Stup
All rights reserved in all media.

Publisher: SarahStup.com
ISBN 0-9788408-0-1

To order copies online of *Are your eyes listening?*,
or to learn about Sarah Stup's other books and special
group discounts, visit

www.SarahStup.com
P.O. Box 1048
Frederick, MD 21702

*No part of this book may be reproduced, stored in or introduced into a
retrieval system or transmitted in any form or by any means (electronic,
mechanical, photocopying, recording or otherwise) without the prior written
permission of the copyright owner and publisher.*

*The scanning, uploading and distribution of this book via the Internet or via
any other means without the permission of the copyright owner and/or
publisher is illegal and punishable by law. Please purchase only authorized
electronic editions of this work to prevent the piracy of copyrighted materials.
Your support of the author's rights is appreciated.*

To all individuals with disabilities,
real people
inside bodies that work differently

Table of contents

Are your eyes listening? That's what needs to happen to hear my writing voice. Because of autism, the thief of politeness and friendship, I have no sounding voice. By typing words I can play with my life and stretch from my world to yours. I become a real person when my words try to reach out to you without my weird body scaring you away. Then I am alive.

With writing I reach out to try, and autism or hate or walls of doubt can't hold me. I am pleased to be typing away—typing away loneliness, typing away silence, using paper to hug you and slap you and join you. Click, click, clicking keys are my heartbeat. Listen with your eyes.

— Sarah Stup

autism,
the experience

The beast called autism

Autism is part beast and part
human with people trying to tame
the naughty animal. The beast has
talent but can't always put on a
good show. The beast scares you and
the human is sad and lonely. Love
my beast. Beast keeps me safe. Find
me inside the beast. I am the soul.

Paths to peace

A naughty beast called autism lives inside, protecting me
from seeing and hearing too much. Even though I hoped
to get rid of autism, I knew I needed the beast to shield
me from a world that pains and confuses me. My autism
protects me when your world is too much for me. Noises
pain my ears and keep echoing. Voices bunch together
sometimes. Ears hear too much. Ears know no peace. Places
scream to me. After I leave, the echo tags along. I hear too
well. Sounds pay me visits after I leave them. I wish to stop
their visits, but they come uninvited.

Acting opposite of deaf, my ears hear too much. Sounds
stay with me long after they are made. They echo and
vibrate through my body. I can't get away from them
except when I pace back and forth quickly and keep the
sounds behind me.

A horrible time is when many different voices are sounding.
When this happens I need to protect myself by doing weird
things like rubbing my nose or ears or eyes. With these
actions I can tune into autism that shields me from noises
and lets me breathe. My body is peace opposite, not feeling
calm or feeling quiet. I found ways to get rid of your
confusing world with my weird actions like touching walls
and licking my fingertips and scratching paper. With these
weird actions I feel calmer but you see rudeness. Say not
that I am rude, but say that I am peace opposite.

My body edits not

My body edits not. It goes
places by itself without
listening to me. To be in
a rude body is awful.

Pacing

I ache and can't find my place.
I am lost. Pacing is a compass
that rescues me. It points to a
rhythm I love to step out and
sounds out where my body is
located. A body that was lost
joins my pace. My mind points
the direction and body listens.
Really wish it would listen other
times. Pacing makes me
peaceful and whole. Real pacing
fan. A pacing kid is peaceful.

Inside world

We want to be with you, but your ways are not our ways. Your world is not the same for us. We must create another bearable world inside your world that allows us to breathe—an inside world that protects us from pain of exposure. With this inside world comes peace, but sad and lonely times too.

Where I need to stay

With back alleys and short cuts, I find my way through really painful times when sounds rip through me echoing hopeless chants about where I need to stay.

Rude actions, sad faces

Autism hopes to please people,
but it acts rude and people hate
rudeness. When they see rude
actions, they are frightened and
sad. When autists see sad faces,
we are alone in a world of nothing
you wish to know. Sad faces shut
doors of love and friendship. Sad
faces are endings. Sad faces are red
stop signs on paths that could
have crossed. Rudeness is not our
intent. No sad faces please.

I am inside.

The words are there; the voice is not.

We who are silent have our value.

It is lonely and sad not to talk.

Being autistic is a battle that stays.

Your world hurts me.

I need autism to breathe.

Autism is awful, but I am not awful.

I act dumb but am smart. Please be my friend.

We can't be friends when you hate autism.

Be an explorer who finds
treasure beyond the strangeness.

Someday we will all be
communicating spirits
and I won't be a spirit alone.

early
writings,
early
impressions

The truth about Sarah Stup

The truth will be told
The truth will hurt
The truth is sad
The truth is startling
The truth will not stop the hurt
     but will protect
The truth is beginning its timely birth.

— Age 10

Grandmas are smiles

I love to see my Grandmas.
They tie their hearts to mine.
They don't mind so much my autism
    but hope I am going to be fine.
I ask for snacks and they give them
    with lots of smiles.
They go to church with me
    to love God with me.
They go to the ocean with me
    to be resting.
They love me
    and talk with happy voices.
I smile to see them
    and hope they live forever.

— Age 11

A Sunday for dear Sarah

A Sunday is a boring day.
A dreadful scoring day
When Dad watches his sports.
A Sunday is a church day
When Sarah and her family sing and pray.
A Sunday is a dead day
When there is no TV.
A Sunday is a wash day
When our clothes are clean and folded.
A Sunday is a silly day
When Dad and Mom tease the kids.
A Sunday is a sad day
When Sarah does not behave.
A Sunday is a happy day
When Sarah does her writing.

— Age 10

Judy

Judy is a Mom
Judy is a friend
Judy does not give up
She believes.
Go to hell World!
I have Judy protecting me
She will find the answers
To a horrible puzzle called
AUTISM.

— Age 10

I love nighty night

I love going to bed
 with much education in my head.
I know about a lot of things
 and my mind is full of information.
Dumb Sarah is gone.
Smart Sarah is here.
Wake up Sarah,
 for the day calls out
 with a great big shout!
Do you understand?
Yes, and I found out how to tell!

— Age 10

Hitting

Hitting is sad and bad
Hitting is good
Hitting can hurt
Hitting can heal
Hitting is trouble
Hitting is protection
I must stop!
Just try, Sarah.

— Age 10

Math

Adding takes me far away
To a place of high division.
I can multiply my intellect
And subtract the unused past.

The process of arithmetic creates
A new area of my mind.
No longer on the perimeter
I become equal with my peers.

— Age 10

My bout with death

My days are numbered
But still they continue.
They go in pain
They besiege no one to understand.
I scream.
I cry out.
You hear.
You reach out.
But there it stays
Ugly and strange and horrible.
I kill it!
You kill it!
But it never is gone.
I ask God
But here it remains.
Stealing life from me and you.
Autism please die!

— Age 10

Autism

It is long, full freight trains of noise
    that empty out in rips of tortured sounds
    that won't stay inside.

It is grating noises
    that hurt me and keep me jumping and running
    without escape.

It is wanting to do regular stuff
    but being trapped inside an evil body
    that acts dumb.

It is reading and typing,
    hoping to have friends
    but being disgusting and lonely.

It is about planning and dreaming about being a writer
    and then thinking it will not be my safety net
    for hope and a future.

It is being partly alive and partly dead.

— Age 13

TEACHERS

Mrs. Benfield

You know much
You hope I behave
You are kind
It will be over
I can make it stop
You do ride it out
And speak I do
Instead of shout
Speak   Speak   Speak
The words are there
The voice is not
I am rude
But I love you.

— Age 10

Happy Valentine's Day, Mrs. Payne

You help
You try
You laugh
You cry
You go along for a ride
To a very strange place
Where I am.

— Age 10

Mrs. West

You say I can
You fix my tears
You hope I will
You fight your fears
You are just too right
I am at the bottom of your heart
Tugging.

— Age 10

Visits to the cabin

Visits can be boring
Visits can be fun.
Visits can be short
Visits can be long.
Visits can be exciting
Visits can be dangerous.
Visits are always different
When we go to the cabin.
I will be glad to visit no more
But Dad loves his cabin.
So I will go with Dad
And he will be happy to see his special girl
At his special cabin.
I will be happy to see fish and trees and snakes
And good fires in the fireplace.

— Age 10

Lovely woods at noon

The mountain was high
    into the sunny sky.
The trees reached tall and straight
    to find the sunlight.
Tops of trees are not visible to me
    because I am looking at the ground
    full of nature's wonders.
To walk among them is a lovely time
    for me to pray.
The chipmunk runs quickly
    to his home underground.
The fish swims up to greet me
    at the lake.
Time to walk on and then to eat
To be returning another day.
I love the woods at noon.

— Age 11

Teacher's Pet

With no voice but many thoughts I was part animal and part human in their school. A school for rejects. A school for mostly silent souls inside broken bodies.

It was a place of fear and music and tears and snacks. It was a place decorated with normality, but dozens and dozens of school buses rounded up imperfection and corralled it there. Later I would learn about stares and words that formed fences around regular schools to keep me from trespassing. But then I wanted to escape this special school. I needed to be at my sister's school instead.

Today I am a high schooler who types to speak, but then I was a kid with autism thought to be a dummy. There were no words or actions coming from my busy body to prove a real girl was inside. My body did what it pleased and hardly ever listened to my instructions. Instead it darted about, squealed, and angered everyone. It repeated actions and could not stop. It jumped from high places and ate dirt. No one heard its silent words that said "I am smart."

"Have a good day, Sarah," said Mom as we hugged.

An adult quickly grabbed my hand to escort me to Miss B's classroom for students with autism, an awful youth robber that caused us to see and hear too much. I was the youngest of seven in her class.

In familiar places we students with autism feel calmer. But we need to look away from people's faces where shining lights and shadows move about causing us to feel dizzy and confused.

"Good morning, Sarah," said Miss B. When she placed her fingers on my chin to force me to look at her face I glanced off to the side. My nose filled with her personal smell . . . of paint brush water mixed with shampoos her students used that stayed on her hands after she touched their heads. I love to smell people, and I know their smells well, but I never wanted to look at their shiny faces.

"Look at me," she said.

Instead I looked at my favorite object, the United States flag with shapes and colors a kid could really trust. The stars and stripes made no unpredictable movements or sounds, nor did they demand anything of my naughty body.

"Say Good Morning, Sarah," said Miss B.

I tried, but the words stayed inside.

"Come on, Sarah. You did it yesterday." Miss B moved even closer. Her voice was much too loud for me and it kept echoing in my ears joining echoes from my mother's voice and other people talking and rustling about in hallways.

To keep breathing I rubbed my nose on my sleeve.

"Stop!" said Miss B, pushing my arm down. "Say Good Morning, Sarah."

"Good Morning, Sarah," I repeated suddenly with perfect speech.

Miss B smiled, but not for long, because I ran like a rabbit out the door and down many hallways where echoes could not follow me.

wishes,
fears,
hopes

Wish and climb

Wishes are the beginning of a happy ending for people with or without disabilities. A wish often escapes or is allowed to disappear. But successful people turn them into staircases leading to a sky with no limits. When people decide to climb even a few steps, they can sit on a wish's tail.

Wishing

Wishing is like quick glimpses
    but not a good view.
It is hopeful
    but not in reach.
It is a piece of thought
    but not a plan.
It is going on a youthful imaginary trip
    but not a real journey.

Wishing is a beginning.
Wishing could also be the end.
Wishing is not real
    but it could be . . .
Or not . . .
Or YES!

Wishes play tag with fear.

Icy wishes

Traveling along the usual path
    are fools who think wishing
        makes dreams come true.

Quick riches are easy
    when wishes quote the latest fad
        in music, hair, or clothing.

Sunny and warm and everyday,
    they are expected and received—
        with only occasional cloudy rejections.

Wishes quiet and everlasting
    are pointing to icebergs
        that entrap desperate souls for ages.

Those with icy wishes keep waiting . . .

Fear is holding me back.
I need to roll forward.

New days

New days are new
opportunities for a winner to
extend yesterday. Past is dark.
Wake up, sleepy Sarah! Rays of
hope are peeking through your
window. Win!

Heal me

Wanting asks!
Time races ahead
    with no answer.
The shy request asks again
Days quickly pass
    with no reply.
Whispered prayers are offered
Nights whisk by
    without response.
Screams seek attention
Hopeless winds flow on,
    ignoring.
Answers quote not a time of healing;
Being free is promised.
Time is a heavy gift.
Wanting waits!

Hope troops along through stop signs.

Hope is my leader
out of a world that turns away.

Hope gathers me in its arms
to go in new directions.

family

Belonging to a family
is like being part
of God's kingdom.

Girls labeled "chicks" stay young

To my Grandmother on her 75th Birthday—

Girls are called "chicks" when they are young
But they are not so bright or kind.
Even though you are seventy-five
You can be a chicken forever!
When chickens are older they are better.
They have lovely hats and jewelry
      and speak about places they will visit
      and friends who are wonderful.
Older chicks always have large families
      full of noisy laughter and teasing.
Chickens of a feather flock together
      to celebrate your special seventy-fifth year of hatching.
Happy years of scratching and picking
      in our chicken yard, Grandmother!

Without Janna

With my sister at home I am happy to
be a kid. Without Janna, though, I hate
parents telling me what to do. Really
hate the nagging. Sad to be the only
child. With too much attention comes
grouching. Parents can be pains.

Empty

Today I am lonely for Janna my sister.
She is a lot busy making a home. I have
my own home that is great, but lonely.

Quitting my home to get married is a good
and happy thing, but now the bedroom is
empty and quiet. The sun stretches across
bare bones and the girl who put on the
flesh of growing up is gone.

My Dad

With a curling cat and newspaper
    you are content.

With a car and long grocery list
    you are caring.

With a snow shovel and lawn mower
    you are tending.

With great chocolate fudge and restaurants
    you are pleasing.

With plenty of great beach visits
    you are joyful.

With a Sunday sermon
    you are renewed.

With Judy, Janna, and Sarah
    you are loved.

Happy Birthday, Dad!

Birth Mom

A time to birth my day
Is Mom dancing to my bed
    with hugs and silly songs
She shines on me.

A time to birth my cleanliness
Is Mom drawing water and fluffing towels
    with stories about a day we'll love
She intrigues me.

A time to birth my curiosity
Is Mom finding books and papers
    with new ideas for me to juggle
She expands me.

A time to birth my voice
Is Mom waiting for slow typing
    with praise and pasted keepsakes
She hears me.

A time to birth my love
Is Mom finding a real daughter inside a shell
    with a rhythm and peace that won't give up
She envelopes me.

With Mom I am alive.

Sustenance

Time spent with many relatives is being filled with the food of life. A main dish of love greets us with voices and messages that seem to get inside, filling our souls with easy to digest warmth and acceptance. The bread of life is our memory of gone but loved ones who seem to be watching as they still live in our hearts. Abundant vegetables picked from fertile soil that is safe and protected by our great country keep our bodies healthy. God gives us the fruit of the spirit if we believe. Dessert is laughter and pure joy that is swallowed whenever we choose to be together. Always thankful for being filled with life, we join together in praising God.

It is so cold outside of Christmas!

Christmas tree

Our tree is beautiful. It stands
in a corner adorned with
memories and lit with hope.
Each year it is both different
and the same. And so are we.

Love has no end. The story of love is the oldest and truest ever told.

nature

Lilacs

With peaceful play we made
with lilac bushes a home away
from adult eyes where we
cooked and swept and
planned. When pans were
donated a kitchen appeared.
When watermelon grew in the
adjoining garden a picnic area
appeared. Lilac encased
dreams. A place where futures
were held in an incubator.
Purple heart and hearth. Seeds
of privacy and comfort. The
beginning of home. Plants
that bent down to children.

Warm message

The sky billows with white lambs
    running in soft blue fields
    that have no fences.
Where leaves lay dry and brittle
    on now warm ground,
New shoots of life push up
    warning them to make room.
Room for the spirit of spring . . .
    Room for promise
    Room for change
    Room for new starts.

The warm message is for every living creature.
Step outside to receive
    this important spiritual address from nature.
A billboard could not be as large as the sky
    or as small as the shoot.
A billboard could not move things
    or move itself.
A billboard could not change instantly
    or stay forever.
A billboard is obvious to you.
Is nature?

Young life wisps about,
Playing in the twisting wind.

Walk for a natural high

Walking is with nature and makes
me feel aware. Air swirling around
and smacking against my skin
lifts me away from silly worries
and makes real problems clear.
Warm and sparkling sunlight
causes my emotions to dance
about opening my thoughts to
new ideas. Marching along keeps
my legs busy and a metronome
keeps time while my mind plays
a melody that can't be captured.

Tail service

With me and backing me up
    is my splendid tail,
A balance keeper
    as I lope through trees.
With me and backing me up
    is my lofty tail,
A rudder to change directions
    as I leap with grace and daring.
With me and backing me up
    is my magnificent tail,
A parachute to slow my descent
    as I drop to lower branches.
With me and backing me up
    is my exalted tail,
A brake to stop me
    as I topple down to safety.

Happy day

Riding along,
Singing a song.

Swinging high,
Touching the sky.

Sliding fast,
Reaching the grass.

Spinning around,
Leaving the ground.

Hanging from bars,
Jumping far.

Skipping about,
Giving a shout.

Having a hopping,
Happy day!

Buds

We walked together one dreary fall day,
Our dinner ended just as the trees' foliage has ended.
The youngest suddenly pointed out buds.
Buds of hope and promise for an unseen future—
Buds sprouting on long, dark barren branches.
Buds that will face winter gales and ice.
Buds that must wait.
Buds that look fragile.
Little sprouts that seem to serve as God's contract with us
    to deliver spring.
Buds that must wait.
Promises in waiting.
We plan another meeting and part till then.

Stars are candles on the altar of our world.

Haikus

Cold hits my warm cheeks
Hoping to waken senses
To winter's harsh mood.

Dead and dry they fall
Blankets to protect rich soil
Till the light of spring.

Back to Routine

Holiday is over.
Back to clocks and work and drudgery!
The idea of meeting routine brings dread.
I must.
I pull and jerk boots onto reluctant feet,
Forcing myself onto the track of habit and duty.
It is chilly.
But my tongue catches a snowflake.

places

Places become holders of beauty
and light up like proud parents.

Trappings

Within my home are trappings.
Trappings that beckon me.
Trappings that both wrap me
tightly and set me free.

Home

Home is mine. It knows
me well and asks
nothing from me . . .
Home fits.

Wishloaf

A place I love is the wishloaf of bread
inside our roasting turkey. Mom and
Sarah break bread into tiny pieces to
fit nicely in a huge bowl to be mixed
with seasonings, celery, onions, and
eggs. Mom stuffs it inside our bird
with wishes for a happy family and
family wishes coming from God's
bread of life.

Bedroom visits

Places old bring me peace,
Autism can rest in their presence.
Places free from voices battling
Places free from faces dancing
Places free from painful people.
Places with patterns
    that fold but never dip.
Places with repeats
    that build but never skip.
Counting only heartbeats,
    not minutes lost;
Measuring only thoughts,
    not noting actions;
Listening to my soul,
    not my broken voice.

Places often visited
    can be trusted.
My bedroom knows my autism well,
It never reacts or is scared of me.

People expect,
     Wanting me to be a fake normal;
But my bedroom knows not to corner me
     into a waiting world.
In my bedroom time synchronizes itself,
Never tiring of waiting
     till mind and body connect.

With sun or moonlit windows
     it watches my autism come out
     to pace and obsess
     and cover me with its shield
     of protection . . .
From people.

From your weary world where pain consumes
Panicked autism finds peace in my bedroom.

Promises ahead

Riding there is like a whiff of it,
>> but not yet . . .
Crossing the Chesapeake is like a preview,
>> but not yet . . .
Passing fishermen is like getting closer,
>> but not yet . . .
Seeing motels and restaurants must mean we're here,
>> but not yet . . .
"Yet" is here when the ocean rolls to bid me
>> to come in and laugh.
I try to keep my balance, but it tugs at me.
I go to my knees
>> and good things seem better,
>> bad things are forgotten.
I am washed of this hard life
>> and there is a whiff of the next life . . .
>> but not too fast!
There is the long ride
>> with bridges and scenery and terrible traffic,
But there is a promise on ahead . . .
>> Not yet.

Wave

The beach pleases me when
powerful waves roll in to meet a
young heart that wishes to wash
away pain of autism. Autism leaves
with the water. But air brings it
back. Really love the time waves lap
over my body. They tell me of a new
life when I will taste the salt of a
free soul. Visit a new world of
painless renewal. A wave of hope.

Ancient rescuer

With no shoes I am ready. Shoes are part of my ordinary
existence. They hamper and restrain me now. To go meet
my rescuer I put my head up and let my instinct take
over . . . I feel part of God's world . . . Part of something
bigger than my life or my autism. Its sense of power
envelopes my soul and it communes with my core; and
the Sarah you thought you knew is gone for now.

My nose fills of beginnings never before considered.
My rescuer is ancient but forever renewing. My lifetime
is but a speck of its witness. Roaring mightily, it absorbs
my pain and traps my fear, freeing my spirit. I run to meet
it but it retreats peacefully.

With its return I become even more certain I need to feel it
about me like God's arm. The huge but tender force knocks
out autism's faulty links to a world made for normal senses,
and I find a peace like I have never before experienced.

No noises echoing, lights and shadows dancing, or
unwanted pokes. I am washed of this world's pain as I
sample the serenity of autism gone.

The ocean is a place where normality is tossed away and
only spirit counts.

observations

Ode to a pot of coffee

Float away woes

Slosh away sleep

Brew ideas

Pour warmth

Steam intimacy

Let's make a pot

Of coffee!

Soft shelter

A coverlet encloses me and makes
me feel warm and cozy as I snuggle
under its soft, pliable yarns that are
loosely woven into a basket pattern.
As I refold the rose colored coverlet,
I can smell the fragrance of soap
that keeps our clothing clean. I
hear the rustling and snapping of
fabric as I try to fold it neatly.
Before I put my source of warmth
aside, I bury my face into its folds
for one last taste of home.

Middle times are special times

Middle is between.

Middle is like the best time of the day—lunch.

Middle is like stuffing in a turkey.

Middle is the cream filling in a doughnut.

Middle is the meat of a sandwich.

Middle is not north or south.

Middle is not young, but not old.

Middle is not top or bottom.

Middle is not black or white.

Middle is not left or right.

Middle is centered.

Reach out with a start

Eggs are cells that are drifting away
Expelled from chickens who don't object
    to sharing with us their special golden gifts.
Often going to homes unknown
Feeding real dopes and even me
To provide energy to act our parts
    in living and giving and learning about life.

One enormous cell—how simple a start!
Each person's fuel for special or not special feats.
Just as we place the egg onto our tongues
We are unsure of what will happen this day.
Eggs really are a beginning of choices we make
    To learn.
        To love.
            To try.
                To give.
                    To forget.
                        To laugh.
                            To go forward.

Mmmmm! Marvelous! M & Ms!

Marching out into my hand
        they mass together
Marked with white monograms.

Meant to melt in my mouth,
        they seem to mimic me
To first manipulate and examine
this mob of man-made miniatures . . .
this mishmash of magic mascots.

A myriad of merry colors
        to mix and match—
Most are Boring Brown
        so I munch them first.
No Regal Red at all makes me mope,
But there are enough Graceful Greens
        for a minuet.
Ornery Orange is mutinous,
But Tired Tan marshals easily,
And Young Yellow is yet a midget.
Many maintain they are mere sugar,
But I am mesmerized!

Ode to ears

Pleased to have you
with me,
Ears,
when I travel about
wishing to keep
my balance.

You have
super
semicircular canals
that allow me to stand
erect.
No others support me
the way you do.
Proud
am I
to travel about
with
stable companions.

Pleased to have you
with me,
Ears,
when I journey through
environments
wishing to
hear.

You have sensational
tympanic membranes
that receive waves
of sound.
You transmit vibrations,
acting
without interpretation
or emotion.
What is received
is conveyed,
welcome
or not,
too loud
or faint.

Proud
am I
to roam about
with
reliable associates.

Ears,
reach out to bring
the world
to me.

Silent exchange

With a pew seat to share
    and God as our friend,
We said, "Peace be with you."
You said it aloud
    and I was silent.
Could you be a friend to a girl
    with no voice?
To find me was not easy.
Even so, I hoped you would find a way
    to talk with me.
You typed and I was not silent
    but noisy with asking things.
Good answers came
    and great stories
        of brother and bird,
            of church and college,
                of autism and forgiveness.
With a pew seat to share
    and God as our friend,
    we said lots.
We shared.

Speaking is who you are in the
world around you. It reveals
you to others. It tells them
what you know, what you need,
what you have to give, and
what you love. Speaking turns
you inside out.

Fill up!

Listen to the stories around you.
Reach out to others to find your own
way. Don't be afraid to be different.
Walk with God. Honor yourself.

In love

With love on our minds,
    we change.
We are filled
    with warmth and wishes.
Our hearts beat out praises
    to our object.
Our gait becomes light and musical.
Our eyes twinkle and dance
    to an inner tune.
Our nose pursues sweet bouquets.
Our ears seek mystical channels.
With love on our minds,
    we improve.

Hillsides are climbed,
but heaven is level.

Life continues forever
into deeper places.

writing

Writing is my way out of a lonely place where only God knows. I feel alive to type. The lid opens and out comes pieces of Sarah, a girl with wings who soars above the place with no hope called autism. I am real when I write. Autism is my prison, but typing is the air of freedom and peace.

Typing Voice

Finally, I found my typing voice.
One day, a really nice teacher
touched my arm when I tried
pointing to pictures and letters.
I felt connected to my hand with
her touch, and my hand started
moving where I wanted. With
typing I became a real person.
When I could say who I was and
what I knew and what I wanted,
I was not alone. With typing I
could choose. With typing I was
intelligent. With typing I was not
an autistic dummy. I was proud to
show that I was real. I loved and
hated and was happy and sad . . .
I could tell these feelings. Quitting
the silence was great. I said wishes
and they often came true.

Autism loses on the keyboard.

I type my gifts.

Someday I will let others know
that silent words can scream loudly.

Words typed win hearts.

Eat my sounds

Whisper to me—
    I will listen.
Ask, ask, ask—
    I see you struggling.
Teach me a way—
    I find new power.
Discover my hidden voice—
    I am alive.
Arm me with sound—
    I am a baby.
Wish to help me?

I eat my sounds with utensils acting like
    Knives cutting away
        at proof that I am a stupid girl,
    Forks piercing an idea
        that I am not a real person,
    Spoons that dip out
        words and sounds I can't stop.

Sound is not who I am—
    It is who you are.
I am a silent voice.

I choose to be not your echo.

You find me lots typing.

To type is my real voice.

Tune in!

Read my words—

    They sound like Sarah, a real person.

Voice

Paper is how my message gets out . . .
Paper is the holder of who I am.
Paper is my ticket out . . .
Paper speaks to eyes that hear.

Where I see myself in ten years

My typing is getting louder and louder
because in print I find eyes that listen and
minds can open. The future pleases me.

ramps
over fear

Ramps Over Fear

Through the ages, differences in appearance, behavior, movement, or ability have been viewed as imperfections. Someone—someone we can't really identify—has led society to believe these are imperfections, not just differences. We have come to trust this old message, and therefore our society has no confidence in those with imperfections. Imperfection is feared and avoided. Imperfection is pitied. Pity sounds like caring, but it is really fear. We people with differences are sad to see fear on your faces instead of friendship.

Yes, you offer help because, deep inside, you care. But society likes to keep a good distance from those who seem to be living a sad life. Society had always chosen to separate itself from those with imperfections and group them together.

Today people with disabilities are included, but the sadness continues since we often do not "belong." To belong means to feel valued as who we really are, so we can't feel good about ourselves if we need to pretend to be normal to have your respect. Many of us will fail trying to be you. We will either displease you or be imposters. Your world is not the same for those of us with differences. We often experience your world in a different way; and, therefore, we may need to react to it in an unusual manner.

Pleasing you by posing as normal is what we would like to do, but some of us cannot. For some of us, hiding our strangeness is painful. For some of us, joining your world disguised as normal cannot happen indefinitely. All people should be allowed to bring their disabilities and differences with them, being welcomed as real originals, not fake copies.

We must create a new, exotic garden where two worlds meet and differences are not feared. We must build ramps to that new garden . . . Ramps over fear of differences . . . Ramps that give access not just to places, but to minds and hearts . . . Ramps to help people trust imperfection and our long walk together. The ramps will stretch past old ways of thinking and feeling into this new, exotic garden.

Ramps will take us to a new place where all that is created is considered good . . . Where beauty is found in love and acceptance . . . Where there is no fear of rejection . . . Where no one is hidden away in lonely corners . . . Where all are welcome in body and soul during their lifetime here on earth.

Ramps can stretch from old ways of thinking and reacting to those with differences to a new generation . . . A generation that goes far beyond building ramps to places and to opportunity . . . A generation that builds ramps over fear of differences . . . A generation that steps into the new garden where all are made from His image and perfection is no longer defined by man.

Acknowledgements

Sarah wishes to acknowledge the following:

God's blessings

Family's love

Beth Mende Conny for editorial assistance

Aaron Notarianni Stephens and The Arc of Frederick County, Maryland, for mentoring, creative writing internships, futures planning and connections

Maryland State Department of Education, Division of Rehabilitation Services (DORS) for training and resources, the Reach Independence Through Self-Employment (RISE) grant, and for help in setting up her publishing company

Jean Peterson Design

Also by Sarah Stup

Do-si-Do with Autism is a delightfully entertaining and thoughtful way to introduce children to the importance and joy of building meaningful relationships with those who have autism and other developmental disabilities.

The story revolves around Taylor, the turtle with autism, who sheds light on what it is like to feel pain from the overwhelming movements and sounds around him. His feelings are especially pronounced on square dance day at school. Filled with dread, he retreats to the sidelines and finds solace in his beloved books. To his surprise, however, his classmates follow his lead and, in doing so, begin to focus less on their differences and more on all they have in common.

To order copies of *Do-si-Do with Autism* or to learn about special group discounts, go to **www.SarahStup.com**.

About the author

From her hometown of Frederick, Maryland, Sarah devotes her time to writing and advocating for people with disabilities. Her mission is to sensitize lawmakers, educators and the community at large to the barriers those with disabilities face in gaining acceptance, not just in the workplace but also in all aspects of society.

Sarah is the recipient of numerous grants including the Reach Independence Through Self-Employment (RISE) program, the Maryland Developmental Disabilities Council and The Community Foundation of Frederick County.

To contact Sarah, order Sarah's books online
or learn more about autism:

www.SarahStup.com
P.O. Box 1048
Frederick, MD 21702